Dehiscence

Elizabeth Decker-Benjamin

BookLeaf Publishing

Presentation by *BookLeaf Publishing*

Web: www.bookleafpub.com

E-mail: info@bookleafpub.com

ISBN: 9789395969468

First edition 2022

DEDICATION

Once again-

I dedicate this book to you, reader.

ACKNOWLEDGEMENT

Thank you to the Oxford Dictionary, for always being a cursory Google search away.

Thank you to Google, for allowing me to access the Oxford Dictionary.

Thank you to Facebook, for mysteriously knowing that I wanted to participate in some kind of writing challenge.

Thank you to my husband, Andrew, for being fiercely creative to the point of inspiration.

And thank you to any and all of you that take time out of your day to read this. It sincerely means the world to me.

PREFACE

My husband wanted me to name this book "Cynical Romance", and I told him "no. I must use a word that is both pretentious and difficult to pronounce". Thus "Dehiscence" was born. According to the Oxford dictionary, "dehiscence" means "the splitting or bursting open of a wound" and is caused by the failure of a wound to close properly. Upon hearing the word, my first reaction was that it would be a lovely synonym for poetry. Other contenders for the title were "Liminal Spaces" and "Passive Aggression".

This collection of poetry is the product of frantically writing 21 poems in 21 days. I've searched through my house for every last scrap of scribbled lines on restaurant napkins and half-started Google docs in order to meet this deadline. I tried to structure this book in a way that the poems flowed together, but ultimately they address different time frames of my life. I talk about the budding romance between myself and my (now) husband. I talk about the grief I did and do experience over losing my mom to cancer. I talk about suicidal thoughts openly, and of a murder in Minnesota that shook the entire country to its core.

This book is an eclectic piece, that's enough of a preface, I think. However this book managed to cross paths with you, thank you for opening it.
And, dare I say, thank you for reading it.

Couldn't Speak

I knew you in high school-
or, rather, of you-
I was the Freshman trying hard
not to look at you: a Junior
who was quite possibly
the cutest thing I ever did see-

Back then, you wore clothes
that hung from you
like the memories I have
of the boy I sat beside

I thought you took the seat
right next to me
because it happened to be empty-
I thought you wouldn't remember me.

Today, my own clothes cling to me
like the lingering impression of the girl
who couldn't speak to him
before now.

Welcoming

I've been writing this
since the day I met you.

You crept into my heart, and we drew
on placemats and napkins,
in my notes and in my thoughts,
on dates and in my dreams.

I wake up, words on my tongue,
I fumble with covers just
to turn the lights back on
and grab a notebook-

Visions of you laughing
your face, your voice
a rugged gentleness-
a self proclaimed ogre
with glasses and fluffy hair.

Your mouth splits into
a guffaw for a laugh
and a smile that rends your face
wide open and welcoming.

A List of Things I Must complete

-Finish painting the kitchen cabinets
-Organize the craft room
-Find a way to cram three person's worth of hoarding
into a three bedroom house
-Dust, for the love of God, DUST
-Self-diagnose (depression, anxiety, ADHD, Asperger's)
-Remember your karma
-Endlessly scroll
-Write a poem, a book, a comic, a memoir RIGHT NOW
-Draft a "Living Will"
-Remind yourself we're all dying
-Finish the cookbook you were planning on making with all of your mom's recipes
-Worry about your cats
-Write an epitaph for the grave your mom doesn't have
-Clean up the urine puddle in your husband's shoes
-Complete the Twenty-One Day challenge you gave yourself in the hopes you would buckle down and finish something for once, only to not

save your draft and lose half of your work like a complete amateur
-Look up the definition of: Imposter Syndrome
-Contemplate what makes a poem
-Look up the definition of: Pretentious
-Listen to your pets caterwauling from the other side of the door
-Look up how many cats it takes to become "the crazy cat lady"
-Clean up the pool
-Figure out how to clean up the pool
-Complain to your husband about the pool needing cleaned
-Offer to mow the lawn and follow that up with not mowing the lawn
-Bemoan the ending of summer
-Buy a thousand-and-one Halloween themed wooden cut outs in anticipation of a paint day that probably won't happen
-Look up the definition of: pessimism
-Look up the definition of: anti-social
-Work out (just kidding)
-Finish something
-Finish this list and call it a poem

There Was Fire In Your Eyes

Kenzie said there was fire in my glasses,
like eyeliner-
I told her what poetry was,
I told her it was an 8 year old
niece spouting words
in a chaotically beautiful way-
we watched the bonfire dance
overtop the visage of family
members, as if engulfed
on the other side.
I pictured myself tossing
fuzzy navels into the inferno.
Her other aunt, my other sister,
I remember her pulling
her own teeth
and cackling when we were kids- I thought,
that was also poetry
laughing through the pain
of blood and bone wrenching
from their resting places.
She's older now, my niece,
a preteen- a bright mind-
my sister too, with children
of her own spouting
poetry at her.

Button Up Horror

I love the fall months-
splotches of tawny crimson
brittle air, horror films.

Specters on the screen
people as monstrosities
blood that drips from lips.

Acceptance of strange
interior darks come out
button up horror.

Carry

Sometimes, I’m going to get
uncontrollably upset
and moody,
and broody,
and you'll be obliged
to hold me through it, but

my grief I will carry.

Boo.

I say
"I don't believe in ghosts."
after claiming to see them
as a child-
corners turned as apparitions
dissipate-
I learned about energy from you.
I learned we all worship
the same God, even if we disagree
on the particulars.
You taught me the names of stones
and encouraged my fossil collecting habits.
Tiny, hard pieces of a past
that I wasn't part of. A kid
yearning for memories
that don't exist.
I had an unearned melancholy.
I believed in you
when you talked of spirits and magic.
I used to follow up our conversations
with fumbling in the dark-
because I knew something was there-
Maybe now I've grown too clinical.
I walk with purpose, especially in the dark,
because I know

that nothing is there.
I watch horror movies for fun,
I don’t believe in ghosts.
But my sisters say you visit them
in their dreams-
your wife says she feels
your angry spirit-
I think it’s just unearned
melancholy-
some more yearning
for a past they can’t be a part of.
The truth is, you’re dead.
You’re not a dream.
You’re not a lingering angry spirit-
and if you were,
Why haven’t I seen you?

We Are All Dying to Meet You

We Are All Dying to Meet You

By the time I was 27,
I had amassed a morbid collection-
a mental list of memories
that weren't my own-
a trove of personal histories-
the knowledge that several
of my friends had also
been suicidal or self-harmful.

A loved one once told me:

“I fell asleep in the middle of the street one night.”

he clarified that he was lying
across the pavement in all
black clothing. Praying to a God
he didn't believe in
that a truck could spare him
the trouble of doing it himself.

I asked another friend
if she had a story to share
and after pondering the question
she replied casually
in a voice that could have
been recalling her breakfast
earlier that day:

“I once carried a hatchet with me out into the woods.”

I call it "death flirtations"
and "the call of the void".

I call it "surviving in spite"
or "surviving out of spite".

I call it "I had to keep myself
from driving directly into
the nearest tree."

She told me:

“I once downed a bottle of ibuprofen.”

He laughed and said:

"I had to make myself puke after taking all my lithium."

She mumbled:

“I walked out onto the train tracks and just kinda sat there for a while.”

She explained:

“I just wear long sleeves to cover them up.”

She sang "The Muffin Song"
and said:

“I was in so much pain that I literally asked my friend to just fucking kill me.”

These are all different
people, they are all living
and they are all dying
to meet you.

Under Pressure

A drop of water
that definitely wasn't a tear
on an otherwise dry face
with a not-so-sober expression-

"You're wife made me cry-
No, correction,
I wasn't crying"

Laughing it off and taking a walk
when normally, I thought,
he'd have given someone
something to cry about-

But, that isn't the M.O.
when he's speaking to family-
and it evidently isn't the M.O
when he's speaking
to his overly-nosey daughter in law.

When it comes to family,
they get too many chances.
the words from them sink
below the skin a bit too deep

reaching in moments lacking
clarity, and become distorted
from alcohol and experience-

Words appear and blend
with the voices of a world
Unfeeling-

The world appears almost
as a figure, as a young man
chasing his son down the street
with a hatchet-

the words of a drill sergeant
in the ears of a military brat-

A tirade of figures saying
that he isn't enough-

Not emotional enough
Not black enough
Not man enough
Not worth enough

You won't see tears at a funeral
but you also won't see
any putting on of airs-
You'll see a suit, a tie,
a mouth formed into a thin line

a chin jutting out-
Eyes behind shades
or fixed on a point
just out of sight-
you'll see an occasional twitch,
a foot that taps,
indicators of restlessness
and a reluctance
to speak.
When asked, his throat fractures
trying to sound out words like

"He was a good dude"

and

"They were taking selfies at his funeral"

If you bother to look,
you'll see a person
stuck under the pressure
and struggling, just to be
Enough.

Air Hunger

There are certain words
and phrases
used in the medical field
that immediately project
a reel of images in your mind.

Air hunger.

With this, I picture clawing
hands scraping the air
that frames a hospital bed,
held at bay by metal rails
and shushing nurses.
In the next reel, I picture eyes
bulging, a sunken chest
visibly surging and heaving-

I picture my mom-
a swollen face and sightless eyes
that look next to nothing
like the woman who taught me
how to make pizza sauce-

But that phantom version of her,
I've only seen it in pictures-

even though she never wanted me
to see her like that-

Certain phrases beget certain thoughts-
they create an unintended
dehiscence.

Going Cinquain

Gone.
Expired, deceased.
Clawing, consuming, eclipsing.
An absence that haunts.
Mom.

There Are Worse Fates Than Death

We have six cells back there-
there was a lot of blood
when we opened up today, it
splattered the floor, the three walls
and dripped from the dog's leg
where he chewed his IV catheter
out from his bandage- red against
the robin egg blue paint chipping
off thin metal bars- wagging tail
a foreign body in his body,
a slow, painful, death already happening.
I stabbed myself with the same
needle that flowed fluids into him.
I cleaned up blood and diarrhea.
This morning, I x-ray'd him. No
luck- his owner made the decision.
But, it didn't feel like mercy.
We walked the dog 10 minutes
before putting him to sleep, and
fur on his back was still
warm, his body still so young.
I have to remind myself that
we could only care as much
as his owner cared. But I
still care, and I don't know
how to stop.

Spiraling

I've been tired and spiraling
around and in between
struggling relationships.
People fumbling to be heard-
battles of self worth
and determining what makes
a person have any-
navigating the depths
of peripheral conversations,
always standing in the liminal space
of empathy-
Oh, so you're an empath?
then you'll understand why
I can't be proud of myself
for being one.
Oh, you have anxiety?
Then you'll understand why
I'd rather talk about yours.
Oh, you have depression?
Then you'll understand why
I'd rather crack a joke.
What do you mean you didn't
know how misery wrecks you?
How it smolders your esophagus
and drops rocks into your stomach?

How it crowds your dreams
with realism and suffering faces?
How a single fucking order of fries
can help you catch your breath?
I can't stand watching
you suffer, a feeling of dread
clouding around my vision
and misting my thoughts
With a toxic mental climate.
I want to suffocate
in a pile of potatoes.
Scoop my brains out
with a melon baller
and replace it with the little grey cells
of Poirot-
Design myself a fashionable gentleman
in the 40's and focus
on solving mysteries, and not
on chronic fatigue
and external anxieties that send me
Spiraling.

Lavender

To any and all
when I'm in a bad mood:
may all of your bubbles burst
into small spurts of lavender
from the confines of thumb sized
amber vials- atomized essential oil
misting reception rooms
and breathed in
by “essential” workers.

Travel Mug of Poison

Alcohol, a poison
that both speeds up time
and makes it's passage
more bearable.

An afternoon,
or a lifetime?

Poison in a travel mug-
a gift from a family member-

Did she know the fate
of such a gift?

Do we fathom the destinies
of items consigned to others?

Thoughts wasted, a mind wasted,
flushed cheeks and passing out.

Bits

How to pour a head on the page
in such a way that it means something

What character can I concoct
to tell the story of myself?

Over and over

Does it matter who is reached,
so long as someone is?

A writer must isolate, but we understand through
experience.
Kill yourself to write with meaning.

repeatedly pour heads from pencils until finally,
finally-
Read.
Does it matter if the process kills you?

8 Minutes and 46 Seconds

After he was murdered
it didn't matter to me
what he looked like, where he came from
whether or not he was "no saint"
as I'd heard in response to his demise-
he was a human being
and he was somebody's son, as he reminded us
when begging for his mother in his final moments.

He was a person, and his name was George.

I didn't think it was controversial
to celebrate in the apprehension
and judgment
of his killer-
I thought we all could agree
after seeing the suffocation of a man
so well documented.

I didn't think wanting justice was radical,
I thought it was American.

I didn't think it was radical
to discuss race openly and honestly.

I didn't think it was radical
to keep society from beating me
until I was black or blue.

Queen City Scream

After the murder,
there were riots
downtown and resounding
throughout the Queen City-
like a scream,
pushed through several throats.

DWB

While the city was screaming,
you were driving
on a late night fast food run
and the nearest McDonald's
was out of commission-

You later told me
it was for seven miles
that she followed you from
that parking lot and pulled
you over on a bridge.

She approached your beat
up Ford Focus with a flashlight
and a hand on her waist. She asked

"Have you had anything to drink tonight?"

and

"You know they're rioting downtown."

Your sweet tea apparently
caused her to almost
draw her gun on you
and your brother.

She said

"You were swerving."

when you both knew perfectly
well that you weren't.
She left, your body intact
and your head shaking.

When you told me, I was angry.
I used the phrase "not all cops"
and followed it up with

"But you almost got shot
over a fucking sweet tea."

You said it wasn't the first
time you were pulled over
for DWB. You laughed, and said:

"They're probably on high alert
because of the protests."

Like maybe she was scared,
like maybe she felt the tension
and maybe she saw it, too,
but was afraid to listen
to the city screaming-

well, maybe she should be
too.

Casual Murder

I think one of my favorite moments
from our late night conversations
exchanged between sheets
and over cocktails
was us contemplating growing
old together-
I said:

"Eighty years old. I think eighty is a good cut off for me."

and you thought for a second,
and said:

"If I forget you, kill me."

I've Loved You Through

I’ve loved you through all of it.
My mom dying, your dad recovering.
A casual pandemic
with latex fingers and expressionless
faces. That shitty apartment
with the biblical amounts
of flooding and mildewed walls.
I loved you when our cat died,
when we paid too little attention
to save him. I loved you
when a “friend” became
a threatening presence.
I’ve loved you while
our families fought amongst
themselves. I’ve loved you through
all the cat pee, the conflict resolution,
the credit card debt, the ripped pants,
our depression, the stress, the hidden
bottles of Jagermeister, the politics, the anger-

I’ve loved you through all of it,
and I’ll love you through
the rest of it.

www.ingramcontent.com/pod-product-compliance
Lightning Source LLC
Chambersburg PA
CBHW051748130826
49812CB00033B/1052
* 9 7 8 9 3 9 5 9 6 9 4 6 8 *